PIANO SOLO

THE HUNGER GAMES
CATCHING FIRE

MUSIC FROM THE MOTION PICTURE

ISBN 978-1-4803-7142-2

HAL•LEONARD®
CORPORATION

7777 W. BLUEMOUND RD. P.O. BOX 13819 MILWAUKEE, WI 53213

In Australia Contact:
Hal Leonard Australia Pty. Ltd.
4 Lentara Court
Cheltenham, Victoria, 3192 Australia
Email: ausadmin@halleonard.com.au

Visit Hal Leonard Online at
www.halleonard.com

JUST FRIENDS

By JAMES NEWTON HOWARD

Slowly

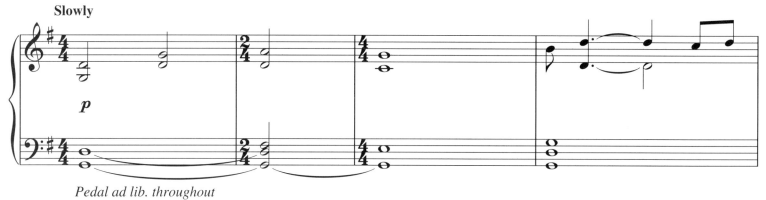

p

Pedal ad lib. throughout

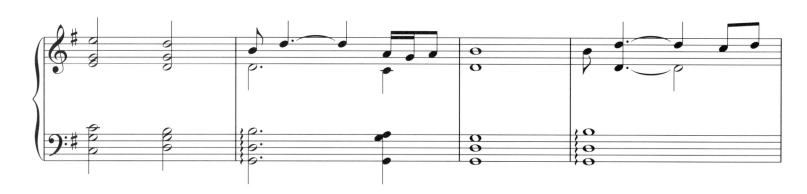

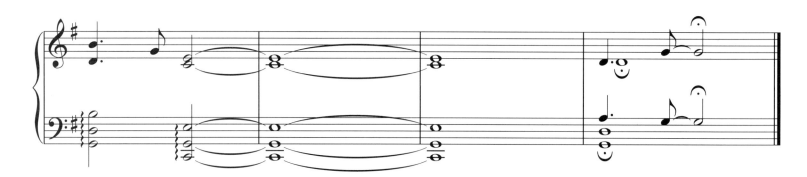

THE TOUR

By JAMES NEWTON HOWARD

Slowly

p

Pedal ad lib. throughout

p

WALTZ IN A
(Op. 39, No. 15)

By JOHANNES BRAHMS
With Additional Music by SUNNA WHERMEIJER
and SVEN FAULCONER

HORN OF PLENTY

By WIN BUTLER
and REGINE CHASSAGNE

Moderately, in 2

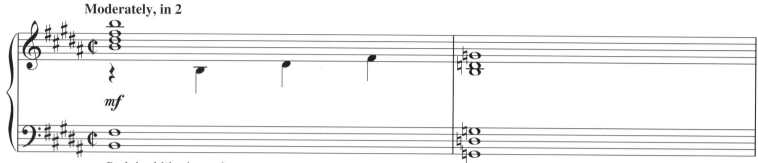

Pedal ad lib. throughout

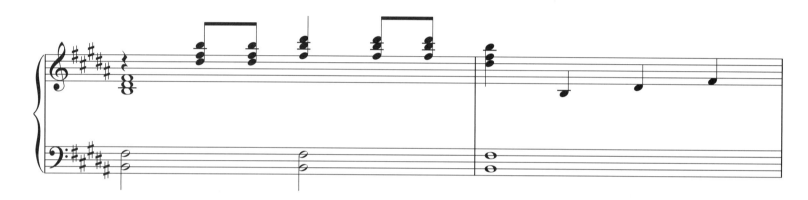

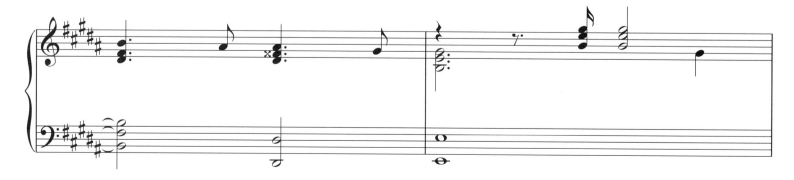

A QUARTER QUELL

By JAMES NEWTON HOWARD

Slowly, expressively

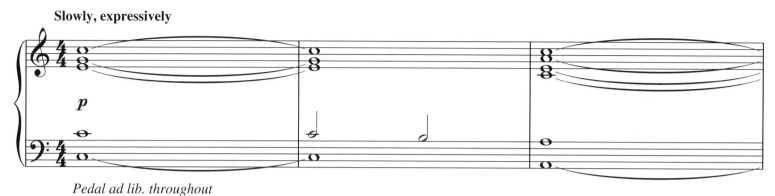

Pedal ad lib. throughout

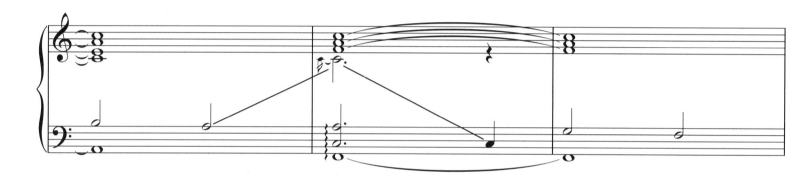

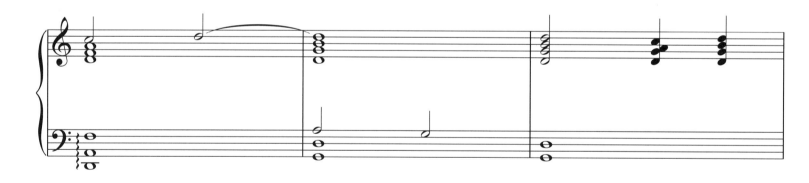

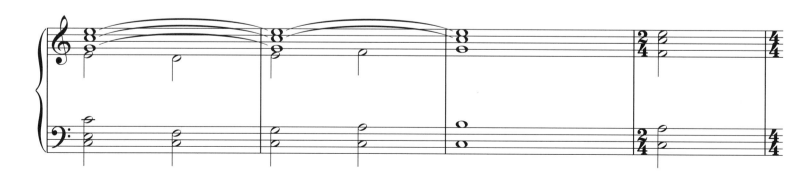

DAFFODIL WALTZ

By SUNNA WHERMEIJER
and SVEN FAULCONER

Moderately

molto rit.

THERE'S ALWAYS A FLAW

By JAMES NEWTON HOWARD

Moderately, expressively

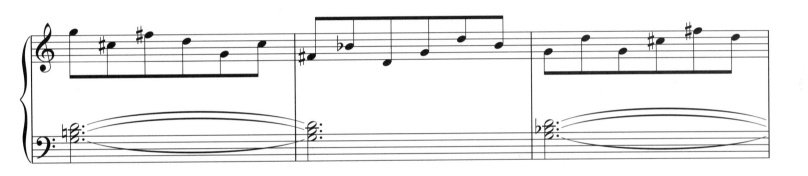

Pedal ad lib. throughout

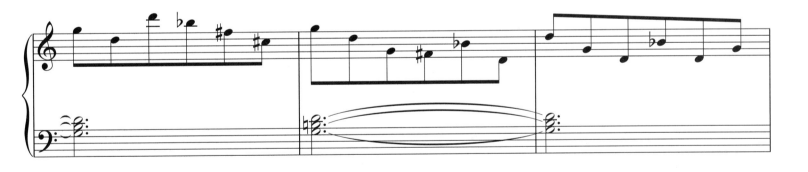

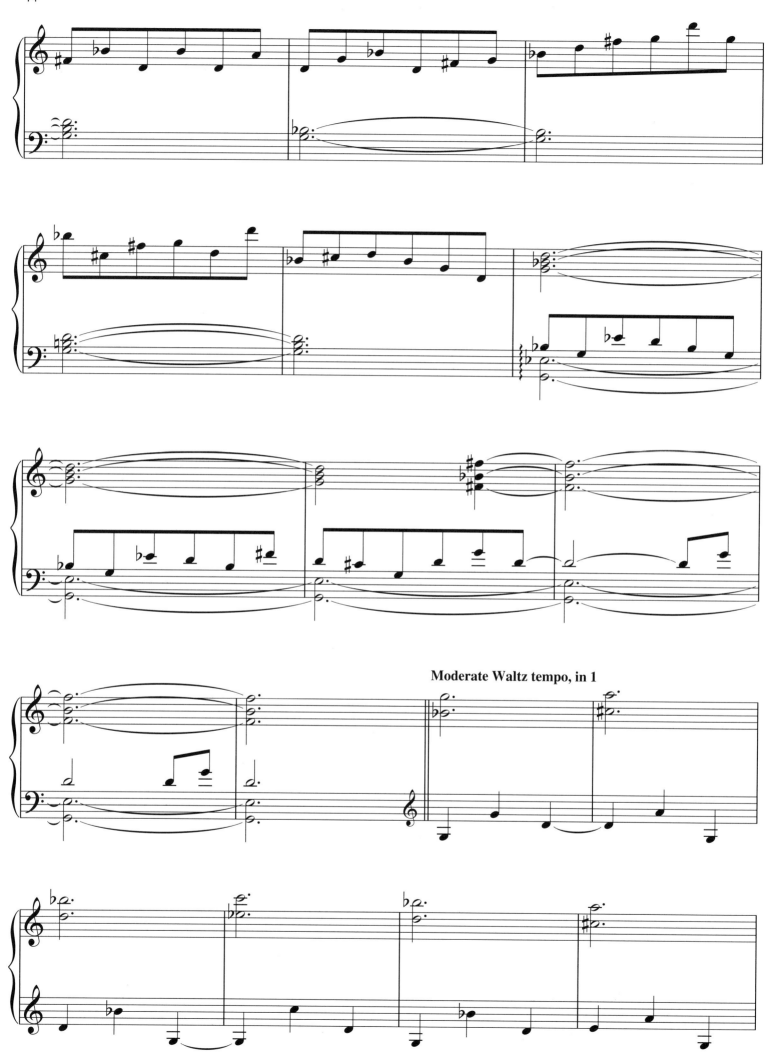

Moderate Waltz tempo, in 1

Moderately slow, expressively

molto rit.

Moderate Waltz, as before

WE'RE A TEAM

By JAMES NEWTON HOWARD,
GUY BERRYMAN, JONNY BUCKLAND,
WILL CHAMPION and CHRIS MARTIN

Slowly, freely

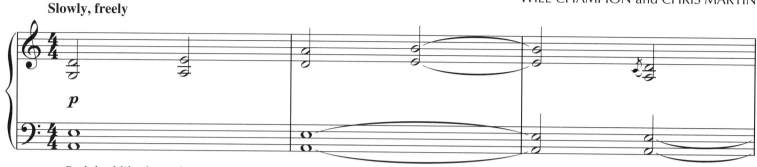

p

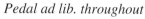

Pedal ad lib. throughout

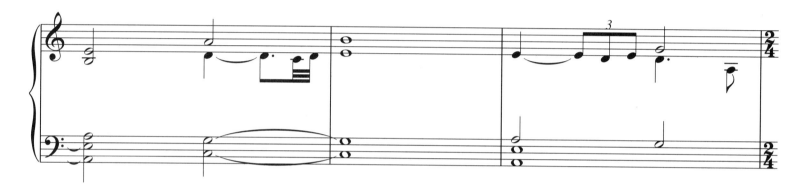

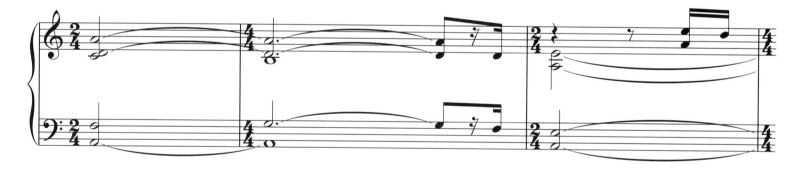

Moderately fast, expressively

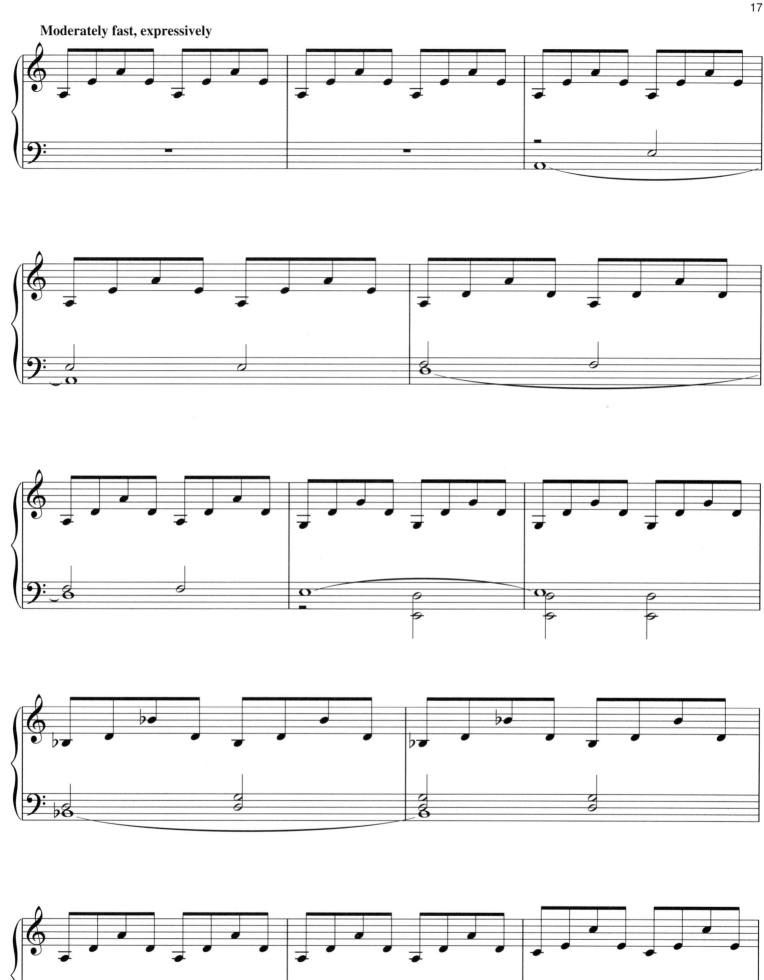

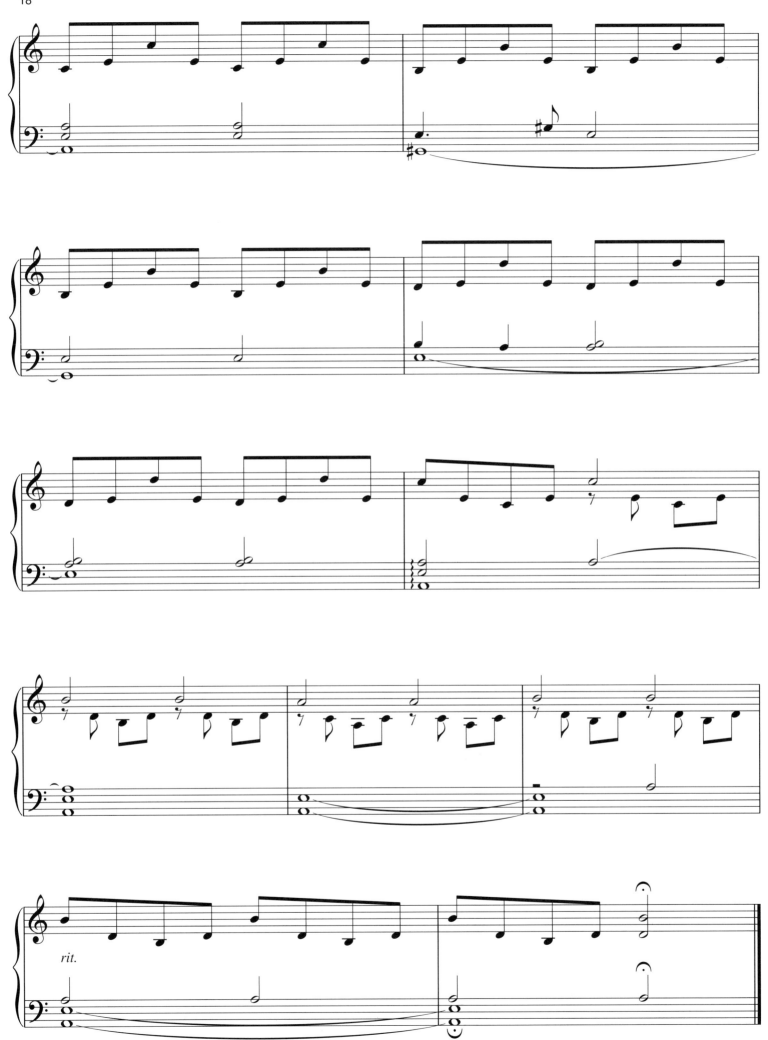

LET'S START

By JAMES NEWTON HOWARD

Moderately

mf

8vb throughout

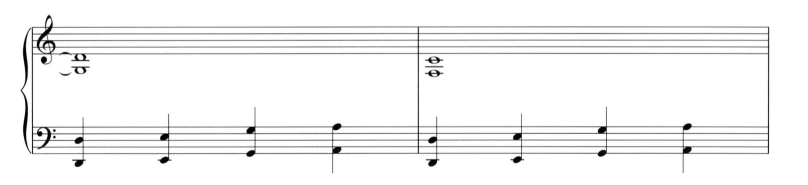

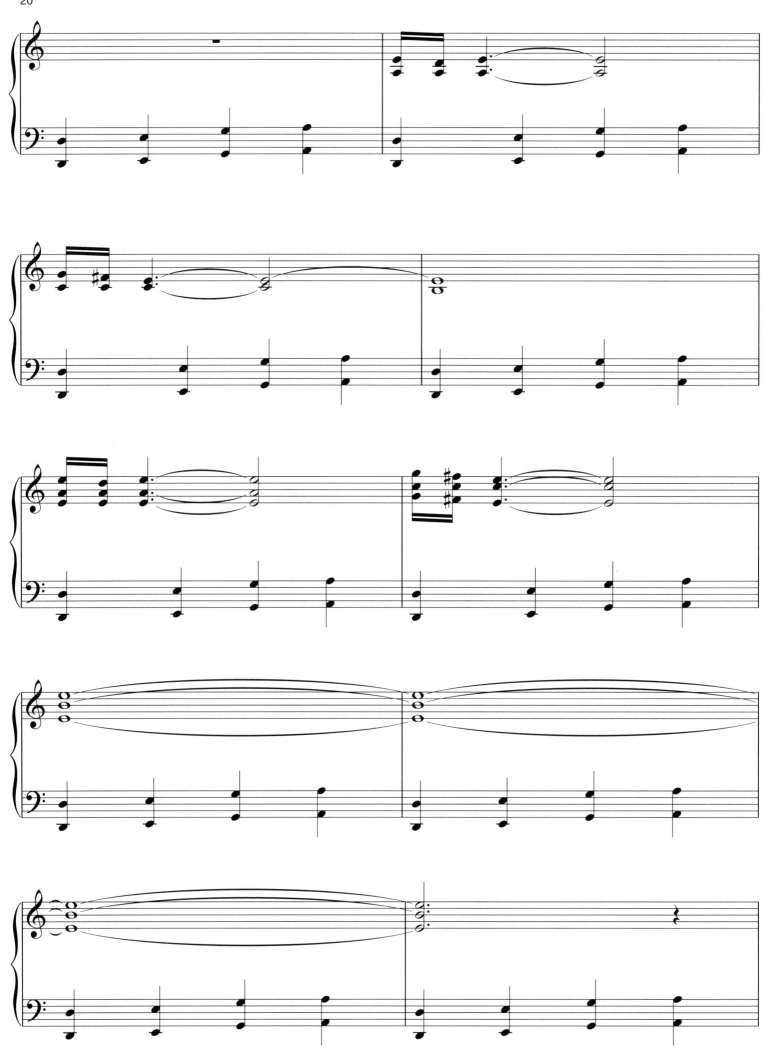

loco

I NEED YOU

By JAMES NEWTON HOWARD

Moderately slow

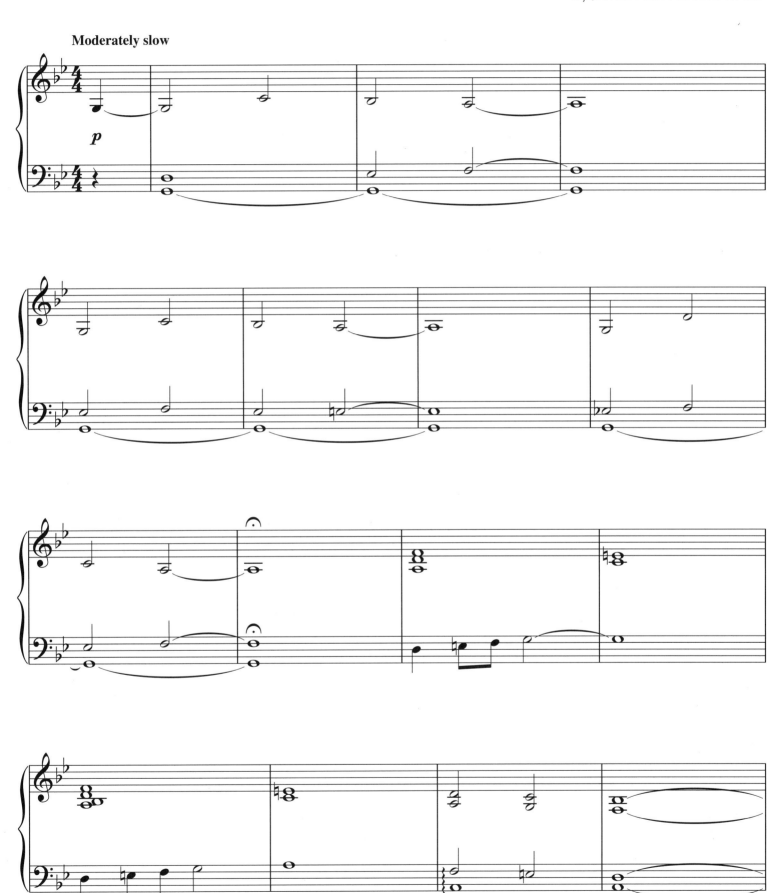

24

Moderately slow, expressively

Moderately

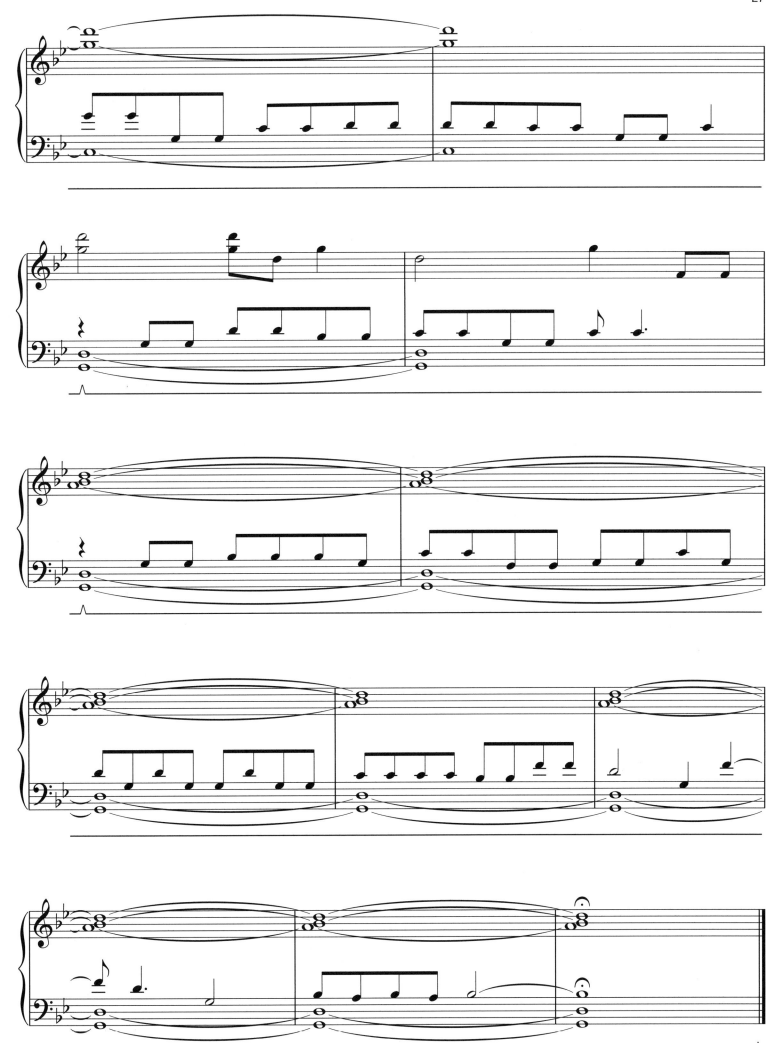

ARENA CRUMBLES

By JAMES NEWTON HOWARD

Slowly, freely

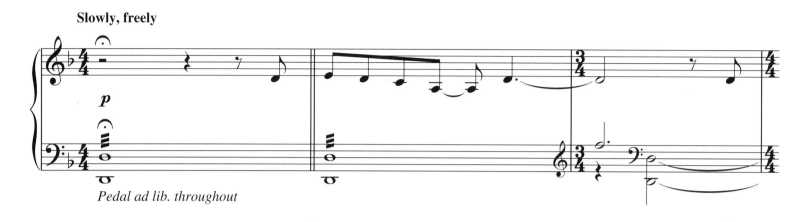

Pedal ad lib. throughout

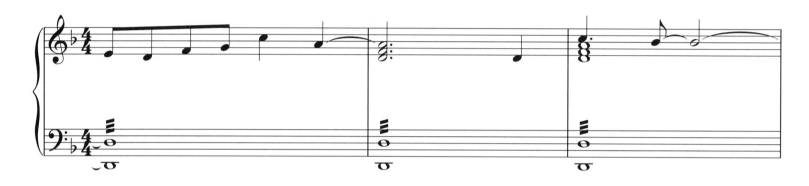

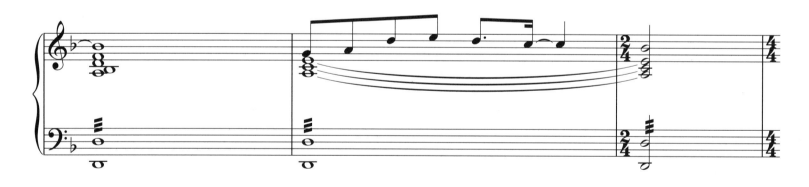

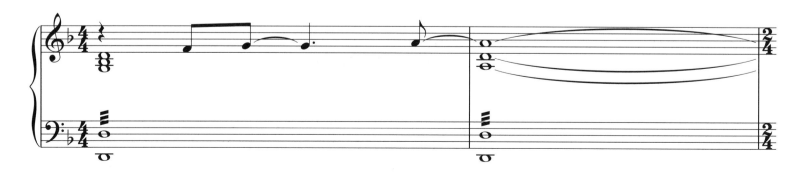